BRIGHT IDEA BOOKS

TEXAS HORNED
Lizards

by Emily Hudd

Content Consultant

Chad E. Montgomery, PhD
Associate Professor of Biology
Truman State University

CAPSTONE PRESS
a capstone imprint

Bright Idea Books are published by Capstone Press
1710 Roe Crest Drive, North Mankato, Minnesota 56003
www.mycapstone.com

Library of Congress Cataloging-in-Publication Data
Names: Hudd, Emily, author.
Title: Texas horned lizards / by Emily Hudd
Description: North Mankato, Minnesota : Capstone Press, [2020] | Series:
   Unique animal adaptations | Audience: Grade 4 to 6. | Includes
   bibliographical references and index.
Identifiers: LCCN 2018058429 (print) | LCCN 2019000090 (ebook) | ISBN
   9781543571790 (ebook) | ISBN 9781543571653 (hardcover) | ISBN
   9781543575132 (paperback)
Subjects: LCSH: Texas horned lizard--Juvenile literature. | Texas horned
   lizard--Adaptation--Juvenile literature.
Classification: LCC QL666.L267 (ebook) | LCC QL666.L267 H83 2020 (print) | DDC 597.95--dc23
LC record available at https://lccn.loc.gov/2018058429

All internet sites appearing in back matter were available and accurate when this book was sent
to press.

Editorial Credits
Editor: Marie Pearson
Designer: Becky Daum
Production Specialist: Colleen McLaren

Photo Credits
Alamy: Robert Shantz, 19; Jack Goldfarb Wilderness Photography: 12; Shutterstock Images: Danita
Delmont, 15, 28, Matt Jeppson, cover, 6–7, 10–11, 20–21, 23, 30–31, Nina B, 8, Seth LaGrange, 5,
SweetCrisis, 24–25, Tessa Easley, 26, YapAhock, 16–17

Design Elements: Shutterstock Images

TABLE OF CONTENTS

CHAPTER 1

A SPIKY
Lizard

See that lizard on the ground? It's hard to spot. It blends in with the sand. It looks spiky. It's a Texas horned lizard!

These lizards are the state **reptile** of Texas. They also live in other western and southwestern states and Mexico. They live in open areas. There are few plants. Their **habitat** has dry soil and sand. They dig into loose dirt. They hide in the ground.

Texas horned lizards live in dry places.

Horned lizards grow 3 to 5 inches (7.6 to 12.7 centimeters) long. Females are larger than males. Both have rough and bumpy skin. They are light brown. They have a white stripe down their backs.

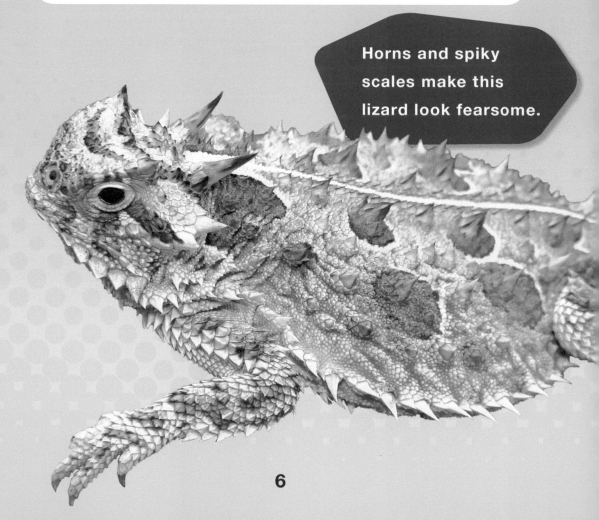

Horns and spiky scales make this lizard look fearsome.

Horned lizards have horns on their heads. They have two big horns on the top. They have many short horns on the sides. Spiky **scales** cover their bodies.

NICKNAME

Horned lizards are also called horny toads. Their bodies are flat and wide. This makes them look like toads.

CHAPTER 2

STAYING Safe

Horned lizards have **adapted** to their habitat. They have many ways to stay safe. They can sit very still. Their colors **camouflage** them in the sand. **Predators** have a hard time seeing them.

A horned lizard is hard to spot on the dry ground.

Horned Lizards flatten their bodies to appear larger.

Blending in doesn't always work. Predators may still find a lizard. So this lizard has a really cool **adaptation**. It makes itself flat. It puffs up its body. It looks twice as big! This confuses predators.

Horned lizards may shoot blood at coyotes that try to eat them.

12

The lizard has another trick. Its eyes can shoot blood! The blood can fly up to 5 feet (1.5 meters) in the air. A lizard uses this trick only on large animals.

The horned lizard's horns also protect it. It thrusts its horns at predators. The horns scare predators away.

CHAPTER 3

LIFE AS A
Lizard

Horned lizards use their surroundings to control their own body temperature. They might need to get warm. So they lie in the sun. Other times they need to cool off. They bury themselves in the cool sand.

QUIET AT NIGHT

Horned lizards are active only during the day. But sometimes females lay eggs during the night.

Sunlight helps keep lizards warm.

FOOD

Horned lizards often eat harvester ants.

Horned lizards eat other small insects too.

They eat grasshoppers and beetles.

The lizards hunt ants in open areas. They look for anthills. Ants remove plants around the mounds. This makes the anthills easy to spot.

Harvester ants are horned lizards' main food.

CHAPTER 4

LIFE
Cycle

Female horned lizards lay eggs in damp, sandy areas. One female can lay 14 to 37 eggs. The eggs are less than 0.6 inches (16 millimeters) long. The mother does not protect her eggs. Baby lizards hatch after 40 to 60 days.

The babies must survive on their own. Birds, snakes, and bigger lizards will try to eat them. The babies are small. They can easily hide.

A baby horned lizard is about the same size as a quarter.

Baby lizards grow for two years. Horns grow larger on their heads. Their scales get tougher. They become adults.

A horned lizard's spikes get harder as it grows older.

Horned lizards **hibernate** in winter.

They bury themselves in the ground.

They sleep from October to March.

They can live up to eight years.

CHAPTER 5

ENDANGERED

Horned lizards were common in Texas.

But now their numbers are going down.

They started dropping in the 1960s.

HORNED LIZARDS TO PLAY WITH

Horned lizards were common before the 1960s. Kids would often catch the lizards. They played with the animals.

Horned lizards are becoming harder to find.

Fire ants are taking over harvester ant territory.

Horned lizards have many threats. Humans are ruining their habitat. The lizards are also losing their main food source. Fire ants are moving in. They kill harvester ants. People spray chemicals to kill fire ants. The spray also kills harvester ants. Their numbers are dropping. The spray can kill the lizards too.

Scientists collect and breed horned lizards to help the species survive.

RESEARCH

Texas horned lizards are disappearing. So scientists are helping them. Scientists **breed** the lizards. They take care of the babies. They let them back into the wild after two or three weeks. It will take work to save the Texas horned lizard. But saving it is important. These amazing animals should live for all to enjoy!

GLOSSARY

adapt
to have differences that help a species fit into a new or different environment

adaptation
a behavior or body part that helps an animal survive in its environment

breed
to produce young

camouflage
to blend in with the surroundings

habitat
the place where a living thing lives

hibernate
to spend the winter in an inactive state in order to survive the cold

predator
an animal that eats other animals

reptile
a type of animal that typically lays eggs and has scaly skin

scale
a type of skin covering found in reptiles, fish, and birds

TRIVIA

1. Female horned lizards are larger than males. They grow to be 5 inches (14 cm) long. Males grow to be 3.5 inches (9 cm) long.

2. Female horned lizards lay eggs at night. Male horned lizards have never been seen active at night.

3. Texas horned lizards can control the blood they shoot out of their eyes. They aim by moving their eye muscles.

4. The Texas horned lizard is the mascot at Texas Christian University. Teams are named for one of the lizard's nicknames: the horned frog.

ACTIVITY

CHANGING BODY TEMPERATURES

Imagine that your body, like the Texas horned lizard's, does not produce heat or sweat to control its temperature. Instead, you need to use your surroundings to control your temperature. You need to stay cool during hot days. You need to stay warm at night. Take a walk around the block or at a nearby park. Pay attention to the temperatures. Are some places warmer or cooler than others? Make a list of places you might go to warm up. Make another list of places you might go to cool down. What makes these areas warmer or cooler than other areas?

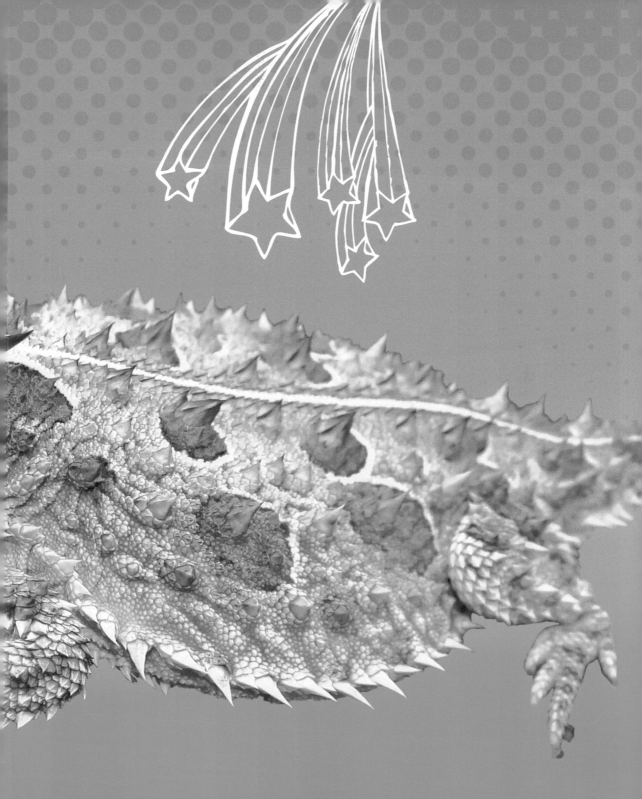

FURTHER RESOURCES

Amazed by Texas horned lizards?
Learn more on these websites:

National Geographic Kids: Regal Horned Lizard
https://kids.nationalgeographic.com/animals/regal-horned-lizard/#regal-
   horned-lizard-close.jpg

Texas Parks & Wildlife: Texas Horned Lizard
https://tpwd.texas.gov/huntwild/wild/species/thlizard/

Ready to learn about reptiles and other animals?
Check out these books:

Hoena, Blake. *Everything Reptiles.* National Geographic Kids. Washington, D.C.:
   National Geographic, 2016.

Mattison, Chris. *Reptiles and Amphibians.* DK Findout! New York: DK Publishing,
   2017.

Wilsdon, Christina. *Ultimate Reptile-opedia: The Most Complete Reptile
   Reference Ever.* Washington, D.C.: National Geographic, 2015.

INDEX